Picture Credits
t=top b=bottom c=centre l=left r=right m=middle

Front Cover Images: Stephenmeese/Shutterstock, kristiansekulic/Shutterstock, Iouriitcheka/Shutterstock, Sergeypopovv/Shutterstock.

Back Cover Images: Rocksuzi/Dreamstime, Iouriitcheka/Shutterstock

Border Images: giangrandealessia/Shutterstock, bouzou/Shutterstock, Eliseishafer/Shutterstock, Morozovatatyana/Shutterstock, Specta/Shutterstock, coko/shutterstock

Insides: Serp/Shutterstock: 6t, Chris Gjersvik/Shutterstock: 6-7m, Ferenc Cegledi/shutterstock: 7t, Stephen Meese/Shutterstock: 8, cbpix/Shutterstock: 10, Phillipdate/Shutterstock: 11t, Jonald Morales/shutterstock: 12-13c, kristian sekulic/shutterstock: 13t, kristian sekulic/Shutterstock: 14, PBfo/Shutterstock: 15t, Wilc Both/Dreamstime: 15b, four oaks/ Shutterstock: 17ml, Davidmschrader/Dreamstime: 18t, XavierMarchant/Shutterstock: 18-19m, Yaniv Eliash/shutterstock: 20t, Musicstyleshoe/Dreamstime: 20b, DebraMcGuire/istock: 21, SashaDavas/Shutterstock: 22l, Dusanzidard/Shutterstock: 22-23m, Iourii Tcheka/Shutterstock: 24, Henrywilliam fu/Shutterstock: 25t, Henrywilliamfu/Shutterstock: 25b, Mhprice/Dreamstime: 26b, diarmuid/ Flickr: 27t, Pietervanpelt /istock: 27b, rpsycho/istock: 28-29t, Janmartin will/Shutterstock: 28b, Lazarevaevgeniya/istock: 29b, Sergeypopovv/Shutterestock: 30, Thomasbarrat/shutterstock: 31t, Dejanlazarevic/Shutterstock: 31b, Lenagrottling/shutterstock: 32, Taiga/shutterstock: 33t, Olga Bogatyrenko/Shutterstock: 33b, Romannikulenkov/Shutterstock; 35b, navy.mil: 36, Jamessteidl: 37b, michaelgatewood/ istock: 37t, Hiroshisato/Shutterstock: 38, Galinabarskaya/shutterstock: 39b, Markinterrante/ Flickr: 39t, Ximagination/Shutterstock: 40, Pavol Kmeto/Shutterstock: 41b, Jarnogonzalezzarraonandia/Shutterstock: 41t

ALL ILLUSTRATIONS MADE BY Q2A MEDIA

Copyright: Really Useful Map Company (HK) Ltd.
Published By: Robert Frederick Ltd.
4 North Parade, Bath, BA1 1LF, UK

First Published: 2008

Designed and packaged by
Q2AMEDIA
Printed in China.

DISCOVER DOLPHINS

CONTENTS

DOLPHINS

Dolphins are some of the most fascinating creatures in the world. Their intelligence and friendliness make them endearing to humans.

 The open sea

WATERY HOMES

Dolphins are warm-blooded mammals that inhabit the aquatic world. They are found in almost every part of the world, with the Bottlenose dolphin being the most widely distributed. They usually prefer shallow waters around continental shelves and some dolphins, such as the Boto, are found in large river systems as well. Each species of dolphin are specially adapted to the area they live in, the food they eat, the predators they may face and the physical challenges they may encounter.

FUN FACT

The ancestors of the dolphins were actually land animals!

There are many species of dolphin in the world and each of them has distinct characteristics and behavioural patterns

LOOK AT US

Dolphins are close cousins of whales and porpoises. They are, in fact, toothed whales belonging to the order Cetacea and the family Delphinidae. They are larger than porpoises and male dolphins are bigger than the females. Their teeth are conical, arranged around a beak-shaped mouth.

The distinct teeth and beak of a dolphin

WE ARE YOUNG!

Dolphin species evolved about ten million years ago during the Miocene period. Today there are as many as seventeen genera with around forty different species of dolphins in them. Different dolphin species vary in size, lying anywhere between 1.2–9.5 m (4–30 ft) in length, and 40 kg–10 tonnes (88 lbs–11.02 tons) in weight!

IN THE BEGINNING

Dolphins are relatively new to this world. They evolved in the Miocene period, around ten million years ago.

The dolphins' spine suggests they evolved from land animals

EARLY DOLPHINS

Dolphins evolved from mammals that once lived on land. They still retain certain land features. For example, all dolphins breathe in air, and some still have remnants of their hind legs. Also, the composition of their spines suggests that their ancestors ran on land and did not live in water.

FULLY AQUATIC

The early ancestors of the dolphin became fully aquatic around thirty-eight million years ago. The Basilosaurus and Dorudon were two such aquatic ancestors of dolphins. In fact, they looked very much like modern-day dolphins and whales, but they still had a long way to go before evolving into the highly intelligent animals we see today. They did not have the 'melon organ' that enables today's dolphins to make sounds. They also had smaller brains. This suggests that they liked to live alone and not socialise, unlike modern day dolphins.

The early Basilosaurus

FUN FACT

Gene tests have shown that dolphins are, in fact, related to the hippopotamus.

ON LAND

The early ancestors of dolphins were known as the Archaeoceti, or the ancient whales. These creatures probably evolved in the early Paleocene period, around 65 million years ago. They were completely land-based. It was only in the following period, the Eocene, that they started living in water more than on land. One such terrestrial ancestor of dolphins is known as the Pakicetus, which resembled the modern-day wolf.

Remains of the Pakicetus have been found in Pakistan

DOLPHIN SONGS

Dolphins are capable of producing different kinds of sounds. Some of these are used to communicate, while others are used to find their way and identify objects.

CLICKS AND WHISTLES

Dolphins can be very noisy animals. They make nasal sounds from airsacs below their blowholes. They make three main types of sounds: whistles, burst-pulse sounds and clicks. The first two are used to communicate with other dolphins. Clicks are used mainly to find their location, identify different objects and see how far they are from them. This is known as echolocation.

Dolphins open their mouths and produce three types of sounds: clicks, whistles and burst-pulses

WHAT IS ECHOLOCATION?

Echolocation, also known as biosonar, is the ability to use echoes to locate objects. Many animals, such as bats, whales and dolphins, use this method. They emit sonar waves, which reflect off objects and bounce back to them as an echo. The time taken for the sound to travel from the animal to the object and back again, shows how far away the object is. Echolocation also helps to determine the size and location of other animals.

FUN FACT

Clicks emitted by dolphins for echolocation are among the loudest sounds made by any animal in the sea!

I CAN FIND MY WAY!

Dolphins produce high-frequency clicks from their nasal sacs located behind a melon-shaped organ in their head. These clicks are then narrowed into a thin beam by the melon and released into the environment, where they hit an object and come back as an echo, which is then received by the dolphin's lower jaw. From there it finally goes to the brain, helping them to find their way.

Bats also use echolocation to find their way

Sound-making Apparatus

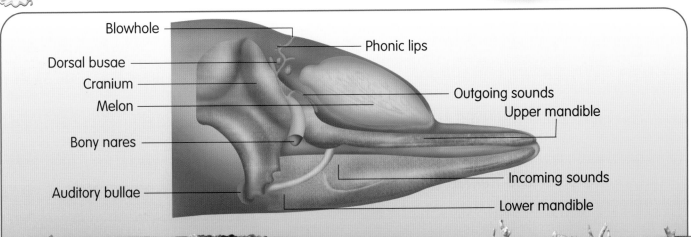

Blowhole

Dorsal busae

Cranium

Melon

Bony nares

Auditory bullae

Phonic lips

Outgoing sounds

Upper mandible

Incoming sounds

Lower mandible

MAKING SENSE

Dolphins use their excellent senses to make life easier underwater. These include hearing, sight and touch.

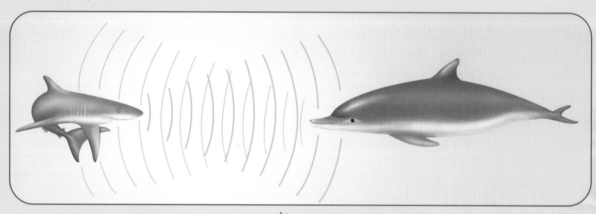

 Sound emitted by a dolphin is received by another in the lower jaw

I CAN HEAR YOU!

The dolphin's sense of hearing is very well developed. In fact, they can hear much better than humans. They have a small ear on each side of their head and their inner ears are covered by a bone called the auditory bulla. Sound enters through a fat-filled cavity in their lower jaw and travels to the middle ear. From there it is transferred to the brain. The middle ear has a large number of blood vessels, which balance pressure when they dive. A dolphin's ears also help in echolocation.

OTHER SENSES

Dolphins also have good eyesight, both under and above water, in bright as well as dim light. Some dolphins, such as the Bottlenose, have binocular vision above water. Their sense of touch is also highly developed. They are known to caress one another as a sign of affection. Although dolphins have almost no hair, they have some hair follicles, which help in their sense of touch.

Dolphins love to eat fish

NOT SO GOOD

The dolphin's sense of taste is not as acute as the other three senses. They do show a preference towards certain fish, but it is likely that this may have more to do with the texture of the fish rather than the taste. Dolphins do not have any sense of smell at all because they lack olfactory nerves.

Dolphins are very affectionate creatures

FUN FACT

Bottlenose dolphins can hear sounds within a frequency range of 1-150 kHz

SWIMMERS

Dolphins are perfectly adapted to their life underwater, from the shape and structure of their body, to what they eat and how they behave.

LIFE UNDERWATER

Dolphins have adapted to living underwater. They have sensitive skin on their lower jaws which allows them to identify small objects, and have a blowhole on top of their heads which enables them to breathe air from the surface. Their eyesight, both under and on the surface of water, is very well developed. With all these senses, life underwater is made easier.

Dolphins have blowholes on top of their heads, which help them to breathe air from the surface

SWIMMING CHAMPIONS

Most dolphins have streamlined bodies to help them move quickly underwater. and their skin secretes an oily substance which enables them to swim through water smoothly. Dolphins also have a complex system of nerves all over their bodies to make swimming more efficient. They have pectoral flippers and flukes, used mainly for steering underwater. Most species of dolphins have dorsal fins.

Dorsal fins help dolphins to maintain their balance while swimming

MERGE WITH THE SURROUNDINGS

The form of camouflage seen in dolphins is known as countershade. Most dolphins are grey, grey-green or grey-brown on their backs. This fades to lighter grey and white on the underside. Viewed from above, they merge with the dark colours of the ocean. When seen from below they blend with the brighter colours of the ocean surface.

FUN FACT
Dolphins shed and re-grow their skin just like humans!

Countershade helps dolphins to blend with their surroundings and avoid predators

BRAINY CREATURES

Researchers all over the world are trying to understand dolphin intelligence. Some believe dolphins are more intelligent than dogs.

HOW BIG IS YOUR BRAIN?

The size of the brain of an animal in relation to its body is a very simple method of analysing intelligence. Big brains in proportion to bodies imply greater intelligence. This ratio in a dolphin is half of that of a human. But, if we exclude the weight of the fatty blubber, then this ratio is much closer. However, it is difficult to compare the brain functions of a water-dwelling animal with that of a land animal because they are designed to perform completely different kinds of tasks.

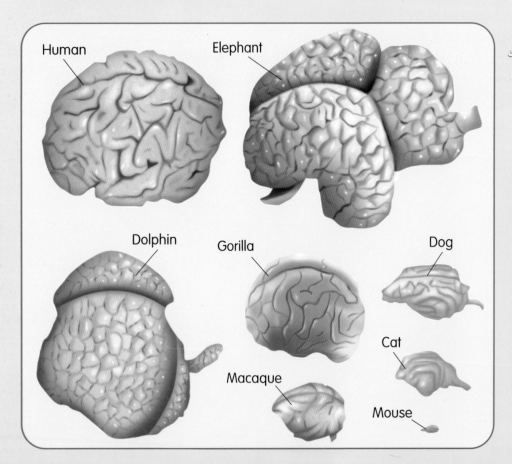

Human

Elephant

Dolphin

Gorilla

Dog

Cat

Macaque

Mouse

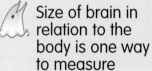

Size of brain in relation to the body is one way to measure intelligence

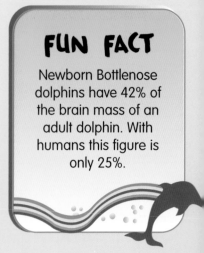

FUN FACT

Newborn Bottlenose dolphins have 42% of the brain mass of an adult dolphin. With humans this figure is only 25%.

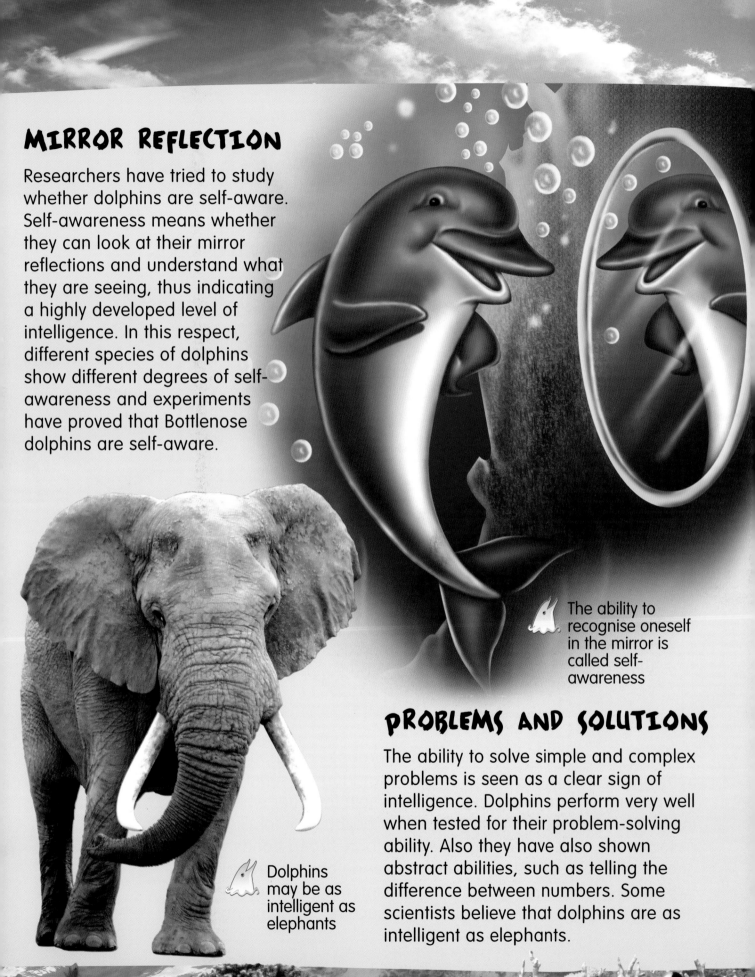

MIRROR REFLECTION

Researchers have tried to study whether dolphins are self-aware. Self-awareness means whether they can look at their mirror reflections and understand what they are seeing, thus indicating a highly developed level of intelligence. In this respect, different species of dolphins show different degrees of self-awareness and experiments have proved that Bottlenose dolphins are self-aware.

The ability to recognise oneself in the mirror is called self-awareness

Dolphins may be as intelligent as elephants

PROBLEMS AND SOLUTIONS

The ability to solve simple and complex problems is seen as a clear sign of intelligence. Dolphins perform very well when tested for their problem-solving ability. Also they have also shown abstract abilities, such as telling the difference between numbers. Some scientists believe that dolphins are as intelligent as elephants.

WE ARE FAMILY

Dolphins are known to have strong familial bonds.
They live together in groups, known as pods.

 Thousands of dolphins join to form superpods.
These dolphins can be seen travelling together

GROUPING TOGETHER

Dolphins are social animals and live in groups called pods. Sometimes, many groups join together and form a superpod comprising thousands of dolphins. Pods join together when they are under threat, are frightened, or because of familial associations. Dolphins in a pod tend to form strong bonds with one another and are known to help other dolphins in trouble. Within the pod, an hierarchy is formed amongst the male dolphins, displayed through behaviour such as tail slapping.

HELLO THERE!

Dolphins make unique whistle sounds, known as signature whistles, to either call another dolphin or identify themselves. Each dolphin's unique signature whistle is developed early in life and closely resembles the whistle of their mothers. Another type of sound they make is called a burst-pulse sound. These appear to depend upon their emotional state, for example, they may squawk or bark when angry and squeak when being playful. These sounds travel into the ultrasound range.

 Humans have recorded the inaudible sounds made by dolphins

CREATIVE ANIMALS

Dolphins are capable of learning complex routines when there is reward waiting for them. Studies into dolphin learning were carried out by a scientist named Karen Pryor in the 1960s. She used two dolphins and rewarded them with food in order to encourage them when they exhibited the desired behaviour. Over time she was able to teach the dolphins a series of complex routines.

Dolphins can be creative. This is seen in the various ways in which they move

MAMA MIA!

Like many living creatures, dolphins protect and take care of their young.

A LONG WAIT

Most dolphins carry their babies for a gestation period of 12–17 months. At the end of this, they give birth to one calf. Although dolphins are capable of giving birth every two years, they usually have intervals of three years. They are known to help one another during the birth of the calves, and help take care of them afterwards.

 Dolphin calves stay close to their mothers. They are often seen swimming next to their mothers, even in large pods

Dolphin calves are encouraged to the surface as soon as they are born, so that they can breathe

MY MOTHER TOLD ME

Dolphins can learn how to use simple tools. Some will use a natural sponge to protect their nose while hunting. This knowledge is passed down by mothers to the young. Female dolphins stay with their pods, but male dolphins often leave and form groups of their own. The signature whistles of individual dolphins are developed during childhood.

BABY DOLPHINS

A newborn dolphin calf is about 1 m (3 ft) long and 16 kg (35 lbs) in weight. In the days shortly after their birth, they have soft and weak tail flukes and dorsal fins which gradually harden over time. Mother dolphins start nursing their calves around six hours after giving birth and may continue for up to 18 months. Calves stay with their mothers for a maximum of six years, during which time they learn how to hunt for food, live in social groups and interact with other dolphins.

Dolphin calves are darker in colour than adult dolphins

DO I SMELL FOOD?

Orcas have been known to come right up to beaches to attack seals

Dolphins use different methods of feeding, and their diet consists of fish and squid.

FEEDING METHODS

Herding is one clever method of catching food employed by dolphins. Here, a pod of dolphins work together to group a school of fish while individual members take turns to feed. Another common method is known as corralling, where fish are chased until they reach shallow waters and are easily captured. Some dolphins, such as the Atlantic Bottlenose, use the strand feeding method. Here, the fish are chased onto mud banks and then can be easily scooped up.

FUN FACT

Adult Bottlenose dolphins eat as much as 4-5 per cent of their body weight daily.

WHERE'S THE WATER!

Despite having water all around them, dolphins don't drink seawater because it is too salty. Instead, dolphins acquire the water they need from the food that they eat. Moreover, when fat is burnt in their bodies, it releases more water.

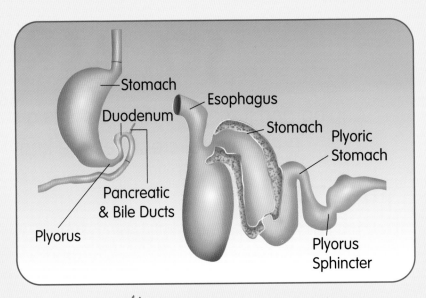

Stomach
Esophagus
Duodenum
Stomach
Plyoric Stomach
Pancreatic & Bile Ducts
Plyorus
Plyorus Sphincter

Dolphins have a special digestive system, which releases large quantities of water from their food

SOMETHING SMELLS GOOD!

A dolphin's diet usually consists of fish, squid and shrimp. The quantity of food they eat depends on the size of their prey. For big fish, such as herring or mackerel, the quantity can be much less than for squid or shrimp. Their stomachs have different compartments to aid digestion. They also have a very strong muscle in their throat, which allows them to swallow their food without taking in seawater.

Dolphins like to eat fish, such as herring, cod, sardines and mackerel

SEA ACROBATS

Leaping and jumping out of water is a common sight among dolphins. These playful creatures are known to be very acrobatic.

PLAY TIME

Dolphins are very playful, intelligent creatures, and are often seen jumping out of the water and performing acrobatics. This behaviour is known as breaching. Dolphins can also be seen riding on waves created by boats or ships. This has probably developed from their natural habit of riding on swells created by whales or swimming alongside their mothers as calves. They are often seen playing, tossing seaweed, carrying objects, mock fighting and chasing one another. They chase other creatures as well, such as turtles or sea birds, for fun.

FUN FACT

A dolphin can jump as high as 4.9 m (16.1 ft) from the water.

Dolphins love to play and are often seen chasing each other

WHAT DO WE KNOW?

Scientists around the world are fascinated by the dolphin's breaching behaviour. Some believe that dolphins jump out of water to view prey from above and to look for signs, such as feeding birds, to help locate prey. The behaviour may also be a form of communication, a sign to other dolphins to join the hunt, and showing which direction they're heading. Dislodging parasites is another possible reason for breaching; or perhaps dolphins leap and jump and spin simply for fun!

Jumping high into the air and then falling on their backs or sides is known as breaching

SPINNING AROUND

Some of the most interesting acrobatic moves are performed by Spinner dolphins. They can jump out of the water and barrel roll. These are small, usually dark grey dolphins, with long and thin beaks. It is not certain as to why these dolphins spin but one explanation is that the bubbles created during spinning helps with echolocation.

Spinner dolphins will often perform several barrel rolls in succession

DOLPHIN FAMILY

The Delphinidae is the largest family among all the Cetacea, and includes many species with different sizes, shapes and characteristics.

WE ARE NOT COMMON

There are two types of Common dolphin – the Long-beaked and the Short-beaked, distinguished by the length of their beaks. Some scientists have also identified a third type of Common dolphin, which have extremely long, thin beaks. Common dolphins can be found all over the world, in tropical, sub-tropical and temperate waters, particularly in the Mediterranean and Red seas. They travel in large active pods of 100–2000 dolphins.

Common dolphins usually travel in groups of 10–50

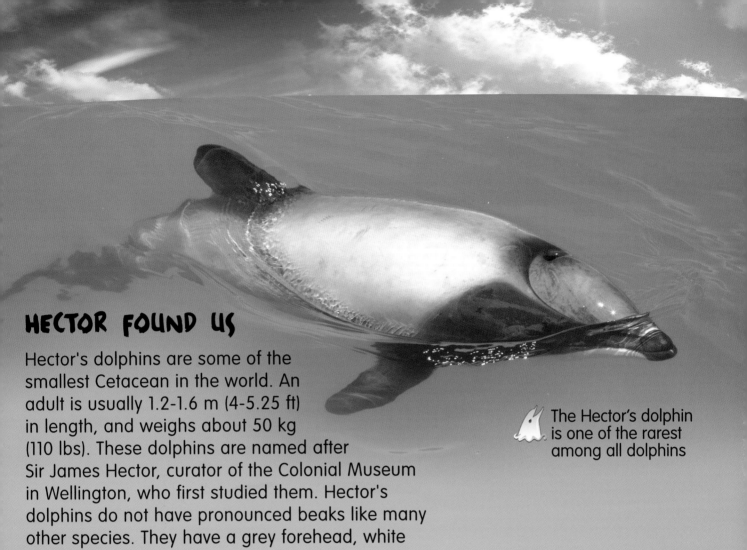

HECTOR FOUND US

Hector's dolphins are some of the smallest Cetacean in the world. An adult is usually 1.2-1.6 m (4-5.25 ft) in length, and weighs about 50 kg (110 lbs). These dolphins are named after Sir James Hector, curator of the Colonial Museum in Wellington, who first studied them. Hector's dolphins do not have pronounced beaks like many other species. They have a grey forehead, white throat and chest and a dark shade of grey running from their eyes to their flippers.

The Hector's dolphin is one of the rarest among all dolphins

Dusky dolphins can cover vast distances. But such movements may have nothing to do with their migration

WE ARE DUSKY

Dusky dolphins are very active and friendly. They are usually found around coastal regions in the Southern Hemisphere and the largest ones have been found off the coast of Peru. They can be as long as 210 cm (82.7 in) and weigh about 100 kg (220.5 lbs). The main danger facing these friendly dolphins is being trapped in fishing nets.

NO KILLER

Killer Whales are actually dolphins and the largest among all ocean-living dolphins. They are found in all the oceans of the world, from extremely warm to extremely cold regions.

BLACK AND WHITE

Killer Whales are easily distinguishable because of their black backs, white chests and sides and white patch near their eyes. They have large, heavy bodies, the largest weighing over 8 tonnes (17,636 lbs) and measuring about 9.8 m (32 ft) in length. It is this bulk that gives them the strength to move very fast. They have been known to move at speeds of 56 km/h (35 mph). Male Killer Whales are usually larger than females. One feature that helps to distinguish individual Killer Whales, is the pattern of white or grey saddle patches on their dorsal fins. Killer Whales are also known as Orcas.

I'M ON A DIET

Killer Whales are opportunistic hunters. Their diet consists mostly of fish, particularly salmon, herring and tuna. Some Killer Whales are also known to hunt sea lions, seals, whales, and even sharks. It is common for them to disable their prey first before killing and eating them. Killer Whales are sometimes called Seawolves because they hunt in packs, much like wolves on land.

 Birds such as penguins and seagulls can also fall prey to Orcas

SOCIAL ANIMALS

Killer Whales are known to be social animals. This can be seen through behaviour such as spyhopping, tail slapping and breaching. Some of them have very complex social groupings. Killer Whales have matrilineal societies, which means there is a single dominant mother and both her male and female young live with her for the whole of their lives. When a few of such matrilineal groups join together, they form a pod. But these pods are not as stable as the individual groups. A group of pods joining together is known as a clan and a group of clans joining together is known as a community.

Killer Whales can be easily spotted because of their black and white bodies

FUN FACT

Different groups of Killer Whales have sets of calls that are specific to them. These are known as dialects.

Killer Whales have complex social structures and live in large pods

HUMAN FRIENDS

Throughout the ages the interaction between dolphins and humans has been friendly and special.

WILL YOU PLAY WITH ME?

Dolphins and humans have always been known to share a friendly and playful relationship. Many species of dolphins, particularly the Bottlenose, adapt well to human company. They can also be trained to perform clever tricks and important tasks. They are studied with great interest by scientists all over the world. The level of intelligence among dolphins is a subject that has long fascinated us.

In rare instances, dolphins have even been known to try to protect divers from shark attacks

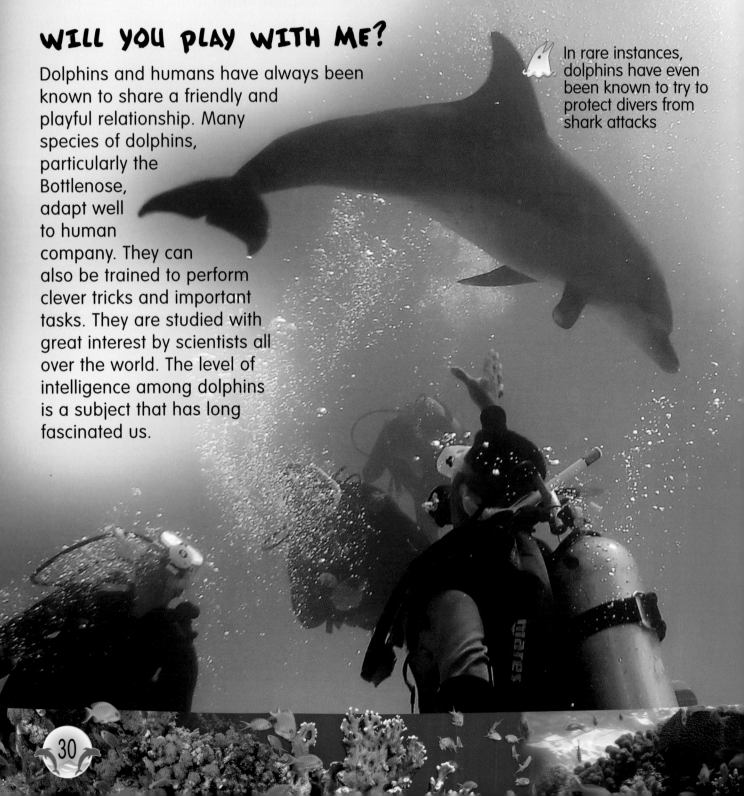

THEY ARE EVERYWHERE

Dolphins feature in the human world in various fields. They are used in the military, in entertainment and in therapy. References to dolphins are also widespread in mythology, as well as literature, art, popular movies and even television series.

Dolphins are even used in therapy

IN THE WILD

It is clear that humans are fascinated by dolphins, but do dolphins enjoy human company as much? Possibly not! Harmful human activities, such as contamination and pollution of seas and oceans with dangerous toxins, have destroyed dolphin habitats and killed many dolphins. Moreover, it must always be kept in mind that dolphins are animals of the wild. So, it is more natural that they would want to avoid human company rather than seek it.

Pollution affects dolphin habitats and ecosystems

ENTERTAINERS

Dolphins feature prominently in different forms of entertainment, such as aqariums, movies and even computer games.

Dolphins are known for their performing abilities

DOLPHIN AQUARIUMS

Dolphins are among the most popular performing animals. People flock to aquariums, where dolphins perform impressive and complicated routines. The most common species of dolphins used for performance are Bottlenose because they live long, look friendly and are easy to train. Some people argue that it is cruel to make dolphins perform for our pleasure. However, there are now strict guidelines as to the welfare of dolphins in captivity.

FUN FACT

In the early part of the 1970s around 37 dolphin aquariums and travelling shows existed in the UK.
Today there are none.

NOT SO SAFE

Dolphin aquariums have been criticised by many on several grounds. Critics say that dolphins in captivity do not have enough space to move about freely, even if the pools are very large. They have also been known to become aggressive and can attack each other, their trainers or even audience participants. Hence, strict rules regulating animal welfare have been imposed, which has led to the closure of many dolphin aquariums around the world.

Dolphin aquariums have often been criticised by activists

The Miami Dolphins use a dolphin as their mascot and logo

MOVIE STARS

Dolphins have been widely popularised by well-known movies and television series, including *Flipper*, *Free Willy* and *The Day of the Dolphin* on the big screen, and *Flipper* and *SeaQuest DSV* on television.

MYTHOLOGY & LITERATURE

Dolphins have long captivated the imaginations of humans. They are a popular theme in mythology, literature and art.

IN ANCIENT GREECE

Greek mythology is full of references to dolphins. Many Greek gods and heroes were rescued by dolphins, including the poet, Arion, the God, Melicertes and the legendary character, Phalanthus. They were also believed to be the Greek sea God, Poseidon's, messenger. They were sacred to the Greeks.

A dolphin is said to have saved the poet Arion

FUN FACT

Dolphin myths help us to understand where they were once found.

OTHER MYTHOLOGY

In Hindu mythology, the goddess Ganga was closely associated with Ganges River dolphins. One such myth tells the story of how the dolphin was one of the creatures that heralded the Goddess' coming down from heaven. The dolphin is sometimes shown as the Goddess' mount, called Makara. In the regions around the Amazon River a popular myth is that the Boto, a river dolphin, can change into a handsome young man!

The goddess Ganga's mount, the dolphin named Makara is sacred to the Hindus

Pots and vases decorated with dolphin images were popular among the Greeks

LITERATURE & ART

Dolphins are particularly popular in science fiction novels, including Anne McCaffrey's *The Dragonriders of Pern* series and a short story by William Gibson called *Johnny Mnemonic. The Music of Dolphins*, by Karen Hesse, is a moving story about a dolphin-human relationship. Dolphins are also popular in art. The Greeks were known to paint dolphins on vases.

MILITARY & THERAPY

Dolphins are intelligent and very trainable creatures,
which is why they are used to serve diverse human purposes.

MILITARY DOLPHINS

 Military dolphins are trained from a very young age

Dolphins used for military purposes are known as military dolphins. They are trained to perform tasks, such as locating mines underwater and rescuing lost divers. The training of dolphins for military use was first started during the Cold War by the USA and former Soviet Union. The US military still runs an open program for the training of military dolphins, known as the US Navy Marine Mammal Program. They were used by the US military during the first Gulf War and also in the recent Iraq War. The Russian military reportedly closed down their marine mammal program during the 1990s.

DOLPHIN PSYCHIATRISTS

Dolphins are sometimes used for the psychiatric treatment of people suffering from depression and for aiding in therapy of autistic and brain damaged individuals. Such programmes are known as Dolphin Assisted Therapy, or DAT.

In 2005, a study involving around 30 people suffering from mild to moderate depression, revealed that contact with dolphins had a positive effect on their mood.

A child enjoys being in the water with a dolphin

DANGEROUS TASKS

The practise of training dolphins for military use has been condemned by many all over the world. It is argued that dolphins come under a lot of stress in captivity. This leads to aggressive behaviour, shortening of lifespan and greater instances of infant mortality. Moreover, introducing them to war zones can be very harmful for these creatures, both physically and mentally.

FUN FACT

The theory behind Dolphin Assisted Therapy was given a new life by Dr. John Lilly during the 1950s and 60s.

War zones can be dangerous for dolphins

HYBRIDS

Some animals are born of parents belonging to different species. These are known as hybrids.

WHOLPHINS

Wholphins are a hybrid of the False Killer Whale and Bottlenose dolphin. Only two exist in captivity. At the moment they can both be found at the Sea Life Park in Hawaii. They are a mother-daughter pair.

FUN FACT

Many hybrids are infertile. That is, they cannot reproduce.

Kekaimalu's daughter, Kawili'Kai was fathered by a Bottlenose dolphin

MOTHER AND DAUGHTERS

The famous captive Wholphin, Kekaimalu, housed at the Sea Life Park in Hawaii, gave birth to a calf at a very young age, which did not survive long. She gave birth to a second calf in 1991, that passed away when it was 9 years old. The Wholphin then gave birth to a third calf named Kawili'Kai, in December 2004. This time she was able to nurse the calf and it survived to adulthood.

Wholphins are very rare in the wild. Only two exist in captivity

IN NATURE & IN CAPTIVITY

Hybrids between different species of dolphin have been found in nature as well, such as the Bottlenose-Atlantic Spotted dolphin and Wholphin. Very few have ever been spotted in the wild, although some may be found in the waters of Hawaii.

THREATS AND DANGERS

The greatest threat faced by dolphins is not from nature but from the cruel hunting methods and harmful activities of humans.

NATURAL THREATS

In nature, dolphins hardly have any enemies at all. This makes them apex predators, or top predators, in their particular habitat. Only some large species of sharks, such as Great White sharks, Dusky sharks, Bull sharks and Tiger sharks, prey on smaller dolphins, particularly calves. Also, larger dolphins, like Orcas, sometimes prey on smaller dolphins. But instances of this are infrequent. Another threat to dolphins from nature are parasites, which cause diseases. Dolphins are usually strong and intelligent enough to overcome most challenges offered by nature.

Great White sharks hunt small dolphins and are one of its few natural predators

FUN FACT

A survey conducted in 2006 revealed that there are no Yangtze River dolphins left anymore, which means that the species is now functionally extinct.

DRIVEN TO THEIR DEATH

In some parts of the world dolphins are hunted for their meat. One method of hunting is known as dolphin drive hunting. Using this method, dolphins and other smaller Cetacean are herded together by boats and then driven onto the beach. Here, they are defenceless and can be killed easily by the hunters.

HUMAN MENACE

The greatest threat to the survival of dolphins comes from humans. Harmful and dangerous practises, such as dumping waste into rivers, seas and oceans, leads to the poisoning of dolphin habitats. Some dolphins perish as a result of accidents with propeller boats. One of the greatest threats comes from certain fishing methods, where dolphins become entangled in the nets and drown. Much of the world has banned these nets, but, tragically, there are still some countries that use them.

 Dolphins can even be affected by line fishing

FACTS AT A GLANCE

- The largest species of oceanic dolphins are Killer Whales, or Orcas. They may grow up to 9.1 m (30 ft) in length, and weigh up to 4,530 kg (10,000 lbs)!

- Some Orcas have 46 to 50 conical teeth, which they use for gripping, tearing and swallowing prey. One male Orca had a dorsal fin 1.8 m (6 ft) long. This is as tall as a man!

- Botos are the largest river dolphins. Adults usually grow to a length of 2.5 m (8 ft), and weigh around 150 kg (330 lbs). The smallest dolphins are called Buffeo. They are found in the Amazon river and weigh about 30 kg (66 lbs), growing to a length of 1.9 m (3.9 ft).

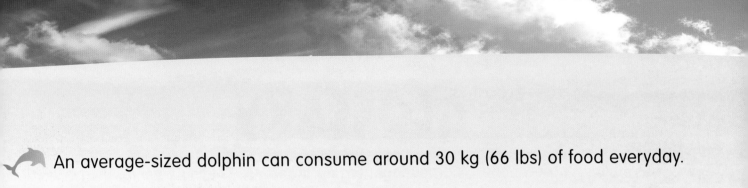

An average-sized dolphin can consume around 30 kg (66 lbs) of food everyday.

The body temperature of a dolphin is similar to a human's at about 37°C (98°F).

Some dolphins are capable of very deep and rapid dives to depths of 305 m (1,000 ft).

Most dolphins have a lifespan of about 20 years. Bottlenose dolphins are known to live for around 40–50 years.

The brain of the Bottlenose dolphin weighs 1.5–1.6 kg (3.3–3.5 lbs).

GLOSSARY

Auditory bulla: A hollow bone that covers and protects the middle and inner ear.

Axis: A line around which a rotating body spins.

Camouflage: The ability to merge with the surroundings so that an animal is not easily distinguished from the things around it.

Contamination: To make a substance impure by mixing it with dangerous and harmful substances.

Hierarchy: A system of ranking people or things according to their importance.

Inaudible: Any sound that cannot be heard.

Infant mortality: The rate of death among the young ones of a species.

Mythology: A set of stories arising out of traditions and beliefs.

Olfactory nerve: The nerves that are responsible for the sense of smell.

Opportunistic hunters: Hunters who take the best advantage of the conditions available to them for hunting.

Streamline: Designed in such a way as to offer the least possible resistance to either air or water.

Toxin: A poisonous substance usually produced by living organisms.

Ultrasound: Sound which travels at a very high frequency. Human beings usually cannot hear it.

INDEX